ALTONA
St. Pauli
Neustadt
Altstadt
Nord
Klostertor
Steinwerder
Kleiner Grasbrook
Wilhelmsburg
Neuhof
Altenwerder
Norderelbe
Reiherstieg
Köhlbrand
Köhlbrandbrücke
Rethe
Spreehafen
Hansahafen
Moldauhafen
Baakenhafen
Rugenberger Hafen
Kuhwerder Hafen
Kaiser-Wilhelm-Hafen
Ellerholzhafen
Roßhafen
Travehafen
Oderhafen
Landungsbrücken
Baumwall
Reeperbahn
Palmaille
Große Elbstr.
Königstr.
Holstenstr.
Max-Brauer-Allee
Jul.-Leber-Str.
Budapester Str.
Ludwig-Erhardt-Str.
Willy-Brandt-Str.
Amsinckstr.
Versmannstr.
Überseeallee
Veddeler Damm
Argentinienbr.
Harburger Chaussee
Hafenrandstr.
Neuhöfer Str.
Reiherdamm
Roßdamm
Georg-Wilhelm-Str.
Reichsstr.
Wilhelmsburger Str.
Köhlbranddeich
Finkenwerder Str.
Theater im Hafen
Blohm+Voss
HHLA Container Terminal Tollerort
HHLA Container Terminals Burchardkai
HHLA Container Terminal Altenwerder
Hamburg Cruise Center (Altona)
Hamburg Cruise Center
HADAG
U-Bootmuseum
Elbphilharmonie
Hafenmuseum
Hansaport
Krusenbusch
Rotehaus
HH-Georgswerder

Der Hamburger Hafen

Zusammentreffen von Groß und Klein: Die großen Containerschiffe brauchen die Anweisungen der Hafenlotsen und die Unterstützung der Schlepper, um ihren Liegeplatz im Hamburger Hafen zu erreichen.

Little and large: the massive container ships depend on the directions of the harbour pilots and the help of the tugboats to reach their berth in the Port of Hamburg.

Der Hamburger Hafen

Ein Porträt · A Portrait

von
Dietmar Hasenpusch (Fotos)
und
Ernst Christian Schütt (Text)

Mit 88 Abbildungen

EDITION TEMMEN

Die Deutsche Bibliothek verzeichnet diese Publikation in
der Deutschen Nationalbibliografie; detaillierte bibliografische Daten sind
im Internet über http://dnb.ddb.de abrufbar.

Übersetzung:
Kristina MacVicar, Berlin

Kartografie:
Tide Verlag Zimmermann, Seevetal

Hohenlohestraße 21 - 28209 Bremen
Tel. 0421-34843-0 - Fax 0421-348094
info@edition-temmen.de - www.edition-temmen.de

Gesamtherstellung: Edition Temmen
ISBN 978-3-8378-5027-7

Printed in Hong Kong

Der Hamburger Hafen

Bedeutendster Universalhafen Deutschlands, hoch technisierte Logistikdrehscheibe für Nordeuropa und Europas größter Importhafen für Rohkaffee - der Hamburger Hafen kann mit vielerlei Superlativen aufwarten. Er ist nicht nur das wirtschaftliche Herz der Freien und Hansestadt, sondern auch Anziehungspunkt für alle Besucher, die auf den St.-Pauli-Landungsbrücken, in der historischen Speicherstadt oder an einem der viel besuchten Kreuzfahrtterminals den Duft von Freiheit und Abenteuer schnuppern möchten. Von hier kommt auch jeden Sonntag von sechs bis acht Uhr morgens die älteste regelmäßige Live-Hörfunksendung der Welt: das Hamburger Hafenkonzert, erstmals ausgestrahlt am 9. Juni 1929 von Bord des Hamburg-Süd-Dampfers »Antonio Delfino«.

Der Hamburger Hafen ist ein Universalhafen, in dem fast alle Schiffstypen vertreten sind und alle Arten von Gütern umgeschlagen werden, und eine Stadt für sich, die niemals schläft und deren Gesicht sich immer wieder verändert. Mit einer Fläche von 7216 Hektar umfasst der Hafen rechnerisch ein Zehntel von Hamburg. Nutzbar sind allerdings nur 6383 Hektar, wovon wiederum 2980 Hektar Wasserfläche sind. Die nutzbaren Landflächen werden zu 26 Prozent für den Umschlag und zu 30 Prozent gewerblich genutzt, insbesondere von der Mineralölindustrie. Die übrigen Flächen werden vor allem für Logistik, Verkehrsinfrastruktur und für Ver- und Entsorgung gebraucht. Die Länge der Kaianlagen und Uferbauwerke beläuft sich auf 52 Kilometer, allein die Kaimauern für die Seeschiffe sind 37,5 Kilometer lang. Gut 320 Liegeplätze stehen für Seeschiffe bereit, davon 38 für Container- und Massengutfrachter mit einer Länge von mehr als 290 Metern. Die Containerterminals gehören zu den modernsten Europas und die täglich mehr als 200 Güterzüge mit 5000 Waggons machen Hamburg zum größten Eisenbahnhafen Europas.

Germany's most important all-purpose port, a high-tech logistical hub for Northern Europe and Europe's largest import harbour for unprocessed coffee - the Port of Hamburg boasts a number of records. It is not only the economic heart of the Free and Hanseatic City, but also a great attraction for all visitors looking to breathe in the scent of freedom and adventure on the St. Pauli Pier, in the historic Speicherstadt district (meaning "warehouse city" in literal translation) or at one of the busy cruise ship terminals. It is from here, too, that the oldest regular live radio programme in the world broadcasts every Sunday from six to eight a.m.: The Hamburg Harbour Concert, first broadcast on the 9th of June 1929 from aboard the Hamburg-Süd Steamer, the "Antonio Delfino".

The Port of Hamburg is a city in its own right as well as an all-purpose port where nearly all types of ship can be found and all sorts of goods are transshipped; it never sleeps and its face is always changing. With an area of 7,216 hectares, the port makes up a tenth of the total area of Hamburg. However, only 6,383 hectares are usable, a further 2,980 hectares are water. Of the usable land, 26 percent is used for transshipment and 30 percent commercially, by the oil industry in particular. The remaining areas are used primarily for logistics, transport infrastructure, utilities supply and waste disposal purposes. The quay and waterfront structures are 52 kilometres long and the quay walls for seagoing vessels measure 37.5 kilometres. There are approximately 320 berths for ocean-going vessels, 38 of which are for container ships and bulk carriers measuring more than 290 metres in length. The container terminals are among the most modern in Europe and with more than 200 freight trains of 5,000 wagons every day, Hamburg is the greatest railway hub of any port in Europe.

Verantwortlich für die gesamte Infrastruktur des Hafens, die Sicherheit des Schiffsverkehrs und die 304 Schienenkilometer der Hafenbahn ist die Hamburg Port Authority. Sie entstand im Jahr 2005 als Anstalt öffentlichen Rechts durch Zusammenfassung der hafenbezogenen Zuständigkeiten der hamburgischen Behörden.

Freihafen verschaffte Hamburg Weltgeltung

Gut 124 Jahre lang, ab dem 15. Oktober 1888, war gut ein Viertel der Hafenfläche zollrechtlich gesehen Ausland. Dies war die Voraussetzung dafür, dass die stets auf ihre Eigenständigkeit bedachte Freie und Hansestadt mehr als 17 Jahre nach der Gründung des Kaiserreiches (1871) schließlich doch dem deutschen Zollgebiet beitrat. Im Freihafen durfte - das hatte sich der Hamburger Senat ausbedungen - angelandete Ware ohne die Abgabe von Steuern und Zöllen gelagert, bearbeitet, veredelt und kommissioniert werden. Dieses durch einen Baukostenzuschuss des Reiches in Höhe von 40 Millionen Mark noch veredelte Privileg des Freihafens trug dazu bei, dass Hamburg bis 1914 zum drittgrößten Hafen der Welt hinter London und New York aufstieg. Zugleich bewirkte der Zollanschluss eine rasche Industrialisierung und den Wandel Hamburgs von der reinen Handels- zur Industriestadt.

Im neu geschaffenen Freihafengebiet entstand mit der Speicherstadt das modernste Logistikzentrum des ausgehenden 19. Jahrhunderts. Dafür wurde eigens eine privat finanzierte Gesellschaft gegründet, die Hamburger Freihafen-Lagerhaus-Gesellschaft (HFLG), Vorgängerin der heutigen Hamburger Hafen und Logistik AG (HHLA). Zwischen 1885 und 1927 wuchs auf Tausenden von Pfählen schrittweise ein Lagerhauskomplex mit einer Nutzfläche von insgesamt 310.000 Quadratmetern. Die Speicher, dem Stil und Geschmack jener Jahre entsprechend im neugotischen Stil aus roten Backsteinen errichtet, boten exzellente Lagermöglichkeiten für Genussgüter wie Kaffee, Tee, Kakao und Gewürze.

Allerdings wurden für den Bau der Speicherstadt mehr als 1000 Häuser und Speicher dem Erdboden gleichgemacht. Gut 24.000 Menschen mussten ihre hafennahen Wohnungen

The Hamburg Port Authority (HPA) is responsible for the entire infrastructure of the port, for shipping safety and for the 304 kilometres of track of the port railway. The HPA was established in 2005 as a public law authority, amalgamating all of the port-related responsibilities of the Hamburg authorities.

Free Port secured Hamburg global recognition

For around 124 years, from 15 October 1888, around a quarter of the harbour area was, for customs purposes, foreign territory. This was also the prerequisite for the Free and Hanseatic City, which was always at pains to underline its independence, finally joining German customs territory, more than 17 years after the creation of the German Empire (1871). In the Free Port - the Hamburg Senate had stipulated this - goods landed could be stored, processed, refined and commissioned without the need to pay taxes and customs. This privilege of the Free Port, which was further enhanced by a building costs subsidy from the Empire amounting to 40 million marks, helped Hamburg to become the third-largest port in the world after London and New York by 1914. At the same time, accession to the Customs Union brought about a swift process of industrialisation and Hamburg's transformation from trading town into a truly industrial city.

The most modern logistics centre of the late 19th Century was created in the new Free Port area with the construction of the warehouse district. To this specific end, a privately-financed company was established, the Hamburg Free Port Warehouse Company (Hamburger Freihafen-Lagerhaus-Gesellschaft, HFLG), the predecessor of today's Hamburger Hafen und Logistik AG (HHLA). Between 1885 and 1927, a warehouse complex with a total useable area of 310,000 m^2 gradually grew up on thousands of piles. The warehouses, built in red brick in a neo-gothic style, which reflected the prevailing tastes of that era, offered excellent storage facilities for consumables such as coffee, tea, cocoa and spices.

However, more than 1,000 houses and warehouses were demolished to facilitate the construction of the Speicherstadt. Around 24,000 people were forced to leave their homes next

verlassen, ohne dass sich die Behörden um ihren weiteren Verbleib gekümmert hätten. Sie mussten sich selbst um eine neue Unterkunft bemühen und hatten nun einen wesentlich weiteren Weg zur Arbeit als vorher.
Als der Warenumschlag in der Speicherstadt immer mehr an Bedeutung verlor, begann hier ein neues Kapitel: Zum 1. Januar 2003 wurde das Gebiet aus der Freihandelszone herausgelöst, damit entfielen auch die Zollkontrollen an den Brücken zur Innenstadt. Seit 2008 gehört die Speicherstadt zum neu gebildeten Stadtteil HafenCity und hinter die denkmalgeschützten Klinkerfassaden zog neues Leben ein. Das Gebiet zwischen Kehrwiederspitze und Elbbrücken ist eines der größten Stadtentwicklungsprojekte Europas und bildet die erste Etappe für den »Sprung über die Elbe«, die Weiterentwicklung der Stadt über die Inseln und frühere Hafengebiete in Richtung Süden.

150.000 Arbeitsplätze hängen vom Hafen ab

Am 31. Dezember 2012 ging auch die Ära des Freihafens zu Ende. Im Zeitalter des europäischen Binnenmarkts und des liberalisierten Warenverkehrs wird so etwas nicht mehr benötigt. Hamburg ist nunmehr ein europäischer Seezollhafen. Künftig können Firmen bei Bedarf für Nicht-EU-Waren eigene Zolllager einrichten. Damit wurden die 17,5 Kilometer langen und gut drei Meter hohen Zollzäune überflüssig. Ihr Abbau und der Fortfall der zeitraubenden Kontrollen an den vier Zolldienststellen an Straßen sowie einer Eisenbahnzollstelle brachte vor allem für die Bewohnerinnen und Bewohner der Elbinsel Wilhelmsburg eine starke Verbesserung der Lebensqualität. Arbeitslos wurden die Zollbediensteten, die im Freihafen immer wieder hochkarätige Schmuggelware aus dem Verkehr zogen, allerdings nicht: Sie halten im ganzen Hafengelände ihre Augen weiter offen.
Der Hafen ist der traditionsreichste, größte und am meisten internationalisierte Teil der hamburgischen Wirtschaft. Mehr als 150.000 Arbeitsplätze in der Metropolregion Hamburg und gut 250.000 im gesamten Bundesgebiet hängen direkt oder indirekt von der Hafenwirtschaft ab, die eine breite Palette von großen, mittelständischen und kleinen Unter-

to the port, without the authorities evincing any concern as to where they would go. They were given no assistance in relocating and now had a much longer journey to work than before.
When 'break of bulk' began to lose importance in the Speicherstadt, a new chapter began: from 1 January 2003, the area was separated from the free trading area, simultaneously doing away with customs controls at the bridges to the city centre. Since 2008, the Speicherstadt has belonged to the newly-created district of 'HafenCity' and fresh life has been breathed into the listed brick façades. The area between the head of the Kehrwieder and the Elbe bridges is one of the largest urban development projects in Europe and constitutes the first stage of the "Leap across the Elbe" - the continued southwards development of the city on the Elbe islands and former harbour areas.

Port provides 150,000 jobs

On 31 December 2012 the Free Port era also drew to a close. This arrangement is no longer appropriate in the age of the European Internal Market and liberalised trade in goods. Hamburg is now a European Customs Port. In the future, companies will be able, if necessary, to set up their own customs warehouses for non-EU goods. This has rendered redundant the customs fences, which measured 17.5 kilometres in length and around three metres high. Their removal and the discontinuation of the time-consuming controls at the four road customs offices and the railway customs office has brought a considerable improvement in the quality of life for residents of the Elbe Island of Wilhelmsburg in particular. However, the customs officials, who regularly prevented contraband goods from going into circulation, did not lose their jobs: they still keep a watch throughout the entire port area.
The port is the is the largest and most international part of the Hamburg economy, with a longstanding tradition. More than 150,000 jobs in the metropolitan area of Hamburg and a good 250,000 throughout Germany depend directly or indirectly on the Port economy, which comprises a broad range of large, medium-sized and small enterprises in long-

nehmen in alteingesessenen und neuen Wirtschaftszweigen umfasst. Dieser ganze riesige Mechanismus dient vorrangig einem Ziel: So viel Schiffe wie möglich so schnell es geht abzufertigen - denn auch hier gilt: Time is money.
Gut 100 Liniendienste verbinden Hamburg mit über 950 Häfen rund um den Erdball - die Stadt ist wahrlich »Das Tor zur Welt«. Die meisten großen internationalen Linienreedereien haben hier ihren europäischen Sitz oder zumindest eine Niederlassung. Die Elbe ist eine der am meisten befahrenen Wasserstraßen Europas. Allerdings ist der Hafen etwa 115 Kilometer oder 70 Seemeilen von der Mündung in die Nordsee entfernt. Der Wasserstand der Elbe setzt dem Tiefgang der ein- und auslaufenden Schiffe somit Grenzen. Aus diesem Grund wurde der Fluss in den letzten 200 Jahren schon mehrfach vertieft. Die Fahrrinnenanpassung von Unter- und Außenelbe ist zwischen Wirtschaftsverbänden und Umweltschützern und zwischen Hamburg und seinen Nachbarländern Niedersachsen und Schleswig-Holstein umstritten. Diese sehen die Deichsicherheit in Gefahr, während Hamburg zur Begründung für seine Vertiefungspläne auf die gesamtwirtschaftliche Bedeutung des Hafens verweist. Ohne weitere Baumaßnahmen können nur Seeschiffe mit einem Tiefgang bis 12,80 Meter den Hafen tideunabhängig erreichen, unter Ausnutzung der Flutwelle sind es einkommend 15,10 Meter.

Der Container revolutionierte den Umschlag

Von den über 10.000 Seeschiffen aus aller Welt, die jährlich den Hamburger Hafen ansteuern, sind mehr als die Hälfte Containerschiffe. Im Zeitalter der Globalisierung ist der 20-Fuß-Container die Maßeinheit des Seeverkehrs und Hamburg mit seinen vier großen Terminals ist als zweitgrößter Containerhafen Europas die Schnittstelle zwischen den Produzenten in Nordost- und Südostasien und den Abnehmern in Nord- und Mitteleuropa. Der Stückgutumschlag, der in Hamburg mittlerweile über zwei Drittel des Gesamtumschlags ausmacht, erfolgt inzwischen fast ausschließlich in Containern.
Jahrhundertelang war Hafenarbeit vor allem schwere körperliche Arbeit gewesen - »Knööv« (Muskelkraft) war bei allen

established and new branches of the economy alike. This whole huge mechanism serves one main goal: to process as many ships as possible as quickly as possible - after all, time is money.
Around 100 regular services connect Hamburg with more than 950 ports around the globe - the city truly is "The Gateway to the World". Most major international shipping lines at least have an office here, if not their European headquarters. The Elbe is one of the most intensively used waterways in Europe. However, the port is around 115 kilometres or 70 nautical miles from the North Sea estuary. Thus, the water level of the Elbe places restrictions on the draught of the ships that can enter and leave. This is why the river has been deepened several times over the last 200 years. The alteration of the channels of the Lower and Outer Elbe is the subject of heated debate between economic groups and environmental organisations and between Hamburg and the neighbouring federal states of Niedersachsen and Schleswig-Holstein, which see the dredging activities as a threat to the safety of the flood protection leveés. The Hamburg authorities, meanwhile, cite the overall economic importance of the port as justification for its plans to further deepen the channel. Without additional adjustment, only vessels with a draught of no more than 12.80 metres can reach the port independent of the tides; using the tides, this increases to 15.10 metres for incoming ships.

Containers revolutionised transshipment

Of the more than 10,000 vessels from all around the world that head for the Port of Hamburg every year, more than half are container ships. In this globalised age, the 20-foot-container is the standard in shipping and Hamburg, with its four large terminals, the second-largest container port in Europe, is the interface between producers in North-East and South-East Asia and customers in Northern and Central Europe. Nowadays, cargo transshipment, which now accounts for more than two-thirds of all transshipment in Hamburg, is carried out almost exclusively in containers.
For centuries, harbour work meant heavy physical labour - "Knööv" (muscle power) was essential for all tasks. At the

Tätigkeiten unerlässlich. Zugleich entwickelte sich ein dichtes Netz unterschiedlichster Berufe, von denen viele eng zusammen und buchstäblich Hand in Hand arbeiteten: Schauerleute, Tallymänner, Ewerführer, Festmacher, Quartiersleute, Kornumstecher - um nur einige zu nennen - sorgten dafür, dass Säcke, Fässer und Kisten von den Schiffen an Land und von Land zu den Schiffen befördert wurden. Der Einsatz von Gabelstaplern machte ab 1952 den Umgang mit der Sackkarre überflüssig, die Ankunft des ersten Vollcontainerschiffs, der »American Lancer«, am 31. Mai 1968 am Burchardkai veränderte die Arbeit im Hafen von Grund auf. Je mehr Güter preiswert und schnell in Containern verschifft wurden und desto moderner die Containerterminals wurden, umso weniger, aber auch umso qualifiziertere Arbeitskräfte brauchte man.

Neben dem Stückgutumschlag ist der Umschlag von Massengut - vor allem von Flüssigladung, Saug- und Greifergut - immer noch eine bedeutende Säule im Hafenbetrieb. Hamburgs Hafen ist auch der drittgrößte deutsche Binnenhafen und hat durch die Wiedervereinigung mit dem Verkehr auf der Mittel- und Oberelbe und den Wasserstraßen Mitteldeutschlands sein natürliches Hinterland wiedergewonnen. Mit seinen Zubringerdiensten im »Feederverkehr« ist Hamburg dank seiner Lage am Ausgang des Nord-Ostsee-Kanals (Kiel-Kanal) der wichtigste Knotenpunkt für die Ostseeverkehre. Fast 50 Feeder-Dienste bedienen von Hamburg aus die Nord- und Ostseeregion.

Kaiser Barbarossa sei Dank

Wie die meisten Welthäfen ist der Hamburger Hafen ein »Wanderhafen«, der sich im Laufe der Jahrhunderte von einem bescheidenen hölzernen Landungssteg unterhalb des Domplatzes an der Reichenstraße und dem mittelalterlichen Umschlagplatz am Nikolaifleet mit den größer werdenden Schiffen in Richtung Elbe verlagerte.

Wesentlichen Anteil am Aufstieg der Stadt hatte eine angeblich am 7. Mai 1189 von Kaiser Friedrich Barbarossa ausgestellte Urkunde. Neben der Gewährung anderer Privilegien sicherte der Herrscher darin den Hamburgern zu, dass sie »mit ihren Schiffen, ihren Waren und ihrer Bemannung von der See bis zur genannten Stadt von allem Zoll und Ungeld« frei sein sollten.

same time, a dense network of different jobs developed, many of which are closely interlinked and go literally hand in hand: stevedores, tallymen, lightermen, lines handlers, quartermasters, corn porters, to name but a few, ensured that sacks, barrels and crates were unloaded from the ships to shore and vice versa. The introduction of pallet trucks from 1952 dispensed with the need for sack barrows while the arrival at the Burchard Quay on 31 May 1968 of the first fully containerised ship, the "American Lancer", revolutionised work at the port. The more goods that were transported cheaply and quickly in containers and the more modern the container terminals became, the fewer workers were required - but they had to be more highly skilled.

In addition to cargo transshipment, the transshipment of bulk goods (primarily liquid cargo, suction cargo and flowable materials) is still an important element of port operations. Hamburg's Port is also the third-largest German domestic port and through reunification regained its natural hinterland and connections with transport on the Middle and Lower Elbe and the waterways of central Germany. Thanks to its location at the exit of the North Sea - Baltic Canal (Kiel canal), Hamburg is the most important hub for Baltic Sea consignments. Almost 50 feeder services provide links from Hamburg for the North and Baltic Sea regions.

All thanks to Frederick I

As with most global ports, the location of the Port of Hamburg has shifted over the centuries. It began as a modest wooden jetty located below the cathedral square on the Reichenstraße and on the medieval transport route at the Nikolaifleet, moving towards the Elbe as ships became increasingly larger.

A deed allegedly promulgated by Kaiser Frederick Barbarossa on 7 May 1189 played a key role in the town's advancement. In addition to granting other privileges, in it the ruler assured the people of Hamburg that "with their ships, their goods and crew from the sea to the town named" they would be free of "all customs and charges". Whether the privileges

Ob diese durch den Grafen Adolf III. von Schauenburg für die Hamburger bewirkten Vorrechte authentisch sind, ist unter Historikern umstritten. Die in lateinischer Sprache verfasste Urkunde selbst, so stellte sich später heraus, ist eine Fälschung. Sie entstand erst um 1265. Damals stritten sich Hamburg und der Erzbischof von Bremen über die Zollerhebung auf der Unterelbe und es musste rasch eine Urkunde her, welche den Hamburger Rechtsstandpunkt untermauerte - mit Erfolg. Da machte es auch nichts, dass dem Hersteller ein kleiner Lapsus unterlief: Am fraglichen Tag war der Kaiser gar nicht in Neuburg an der Donau, sondern stellte in Regensburg ein Heer für seinen geplanten Kreuzzug auf, von dem er nicht mehr zurückkehrte, und das verwendete Siegel ist das seines Enkels Friedrich II., der von 1212 bis 1250 herrschte.
Nun war allerdings die Fälschung von Urkunden im Mittelalter nichts Ungewöhnliches - der Zweck heiligte eben die Mittel. Somit gilt der 7. Mai 1189 als die Geburtsstunde des Hamburger Hafens, die alljährlich beim Hafengeburtstag gefeiert wird. Hamburg wuchs und gedieh und wurde zu einem führenden Mitglied im Städtebund der Hanse. Auch den gefürchteten Seeräuber Klaus Störtebeker brachten die Hamburger zur Strecke: Am 20. Oktober 1401 wurde er gemeinsam mit seinen gefangenen Kumpanen auf dem Grasbrook vor den Toren der Stadt in der heutigen HafenCity enthauptet.

Die Moderne begann am Sandtorkai

Die beträchtliche Ausweitung des Warenverkehrs von und nach Hamburg sorgte in den folgenden Jahren für eine Verlagerung des Hafens in die Elbe hinein. Im 18. Jahrhundert bildeten der Binnen- und Niederhafen (für Seeschiffe) und der weiter östlich gelegene Oberhafen (für Binnenschiffe) die wichtigsten Umschlagzentren. Als 1783 das erste hamburgische Schiff Häfen in den Vereinigten Staaten von Amerika ansteuerte und zu Beginn des 19. Jahrhunderts auch die von Spanien unabhängig gewordenen Staaten in Mittel- und Südamerika als neue und wichtige Handelspartner auftraten, mussten grundsätzliche Entscheidungen über den künftigen Hafenausbau getroffen werden. 1858 erfolgte der Beschluss für einen offenen, jederzeit zugänglichen Tidehafen und gegen

granted to the people of Hamburg by Count Adolf III of Schauenburg are indeed authentic is the subject of debate among historians. It later transpired that the deed itself, written in Latin, is a forgery and was not actually written until 1265. At that time, Hamburg and the Archbishop of Bremen were in dispute regarding the charge of customs on the Lower Elbe and a deed was urgently needed to underpin Hamburg's legal position - with success. It was of little import that the forger made a small error: on the date in question, the Kaiser was not actually in Neuburg an der Donau, but rather in Regensburg, where he was gathering an army for his planned crusade, from which he never returned. The seal is that of his grandson, Friedrich II, who ruled from 1212 until 1250.
However, the falsification of deeds was not uncommon in the Middle Ages - the end justified the means. Thus, 7 May 1189 is deemed the birth hour of the Hamburg Port, and is celebrated every year at the port's birthday celebrations. Hamburg grew and flourished to become a leading Hanseatic League member. It was also the people of Hamburg who brought about the downfall of the notorious pirate Klaus Störtebeker on 20 October 1401. Together with his cohorts he was beheaded at the Grasbrook before the city gates, in what is today HafenCity.

The Modern Age began at the Sandtor Quay

The considerable expansion of the trade in goods to and from Hamburg resulted in subsequent years in the port being relocated onto the Elbe. In the 18th century, the inland port and Niederhafen (for seagoing vessels) and the upper port, located further East (for inland waterway vessels), represented the most important transit centres. In 1783, the first Hamburg-built ship set sail for ports in the United States. At the beginning of the 19th century the countries of Central and South America, which had by that time gained independence from Spain, appeared as important new trading partners. This demanded fundamental decisions regarding the future expansion of the port. In 1858 it was decided to create an open port that could be accessed at all times,

einen Dockhafen mit Schleusen nach dem Vorbild Londons – trotz eines Tidenhubs von damals schon etwa 2,20 Metern zwischen Hoch- und Niedrigwasser. Mit der Eröffnung des Sandtorhafens, des ersten künstlich geschaffenen Hafenbeckens, begann am 11. August 1866 der moderne Kaiumschlag. Bis dahin mussten die Schiffe an Duckdalben im Strom festmachen, dann wurde das Transportgut auf Schuten oder Ewer umgeladen und an Land gebracht. Nun konnte die Ladung direkt mit dampf- und später auch elektrisch angetriebenen Kränen am Kai gelöscht, dann auf die Eisenbahn bzw. Pferdefuhrwerke aufgeladen oder kurzzeitig in Schuppen gelagert, sortiert und bearbeitet werden. Der Sandtorhafen mit dem Sandtorkai und dem gegenüberliegenden Kaiserkai (1872) wurde zum Prototyp des technisierten Umschlags, ihm verdankte Hamburg seinen Ruf als schneller Hafen mit kurzen Liegezeiten. Zudem erhielt die Stadt am 1. Dezember 1872 mit dem Brückenschlag über die Norder- und Süderelbe Anschluss an das west- und süddeutsche Eisenbahnnetz.

Erst mit dem Ende des klassischen Stückgutumschlags infolge der Containerisierung verlor der Sandtorhafen endgültig seine Bedeutung. An dieser Keimzelle des modernen Hafenumschlags entstand am 20. September 2008 ein weiterer Anleger für Traditionsschiffe neben dem Museumshafen Oevelgönne. Die Zeit der Segelschiffe und Dampfschiffe wird hier wieder lebendig, während gleichzeitig der pulsierende Welthafen dafür sorgt, dass Hamburg seine selbstgestellte, 1952 in der Verfassung verankerte Aufgabe erfüllen kann, im »Geiste des Friedens eine Mittlerin zwischen allen Erdteilen und Völkern der Welt« zu sein.

rather than a dock port with a lock system in the style of the Port of London – despite a tidal range of around 2.20 metres. With the opening of the Sandtorhafen, the first man-made port basin on 11 August 1866, modern quay-based transshipment began. Until then, the ships had to moor at anchorages in the river itself, and the cargo was reloaded onto barges or rowing boats to be transported ashore. Now, loading and unloading could be carried out directly at the quayside, initially using steam-powered and, later, electric cranes, before being loaded onto trains or horse-drawn carts or temporarily stored in transit sheds, sorted and processed. The Sandtorhafen with the Sandtor Quay and the Kaiser Quay (1872) on the opposite side became the prototype of high-tech transshipment, through which Hamburg gained its reputation as a port with short turnaround times. Furthermore, with the opening on 1 December 1872 of the bridge over the North and South Elbe, the city was connected to the West-German and Southern German railway networks.

Only with the end of traditional cargo transshipment as a result of the widespread introduction of container ships did the Sandtorhafen lose its important status. It was here, at what is perhaps the birthplace of modern port transshipment, that a new jetty for historic sailing ships was created on 20 September 2008 next to the Museum Harbour of Oevelgönne. The museum brings back to life the age of sailing ships and steamers, while the lively global port ensures that Hamburg can continue to fulfil its task, as set out in the constitution in 1952, of acting “in the interests of freedom as a mediator between all parts and peoples of the world”.

»Willkommen in Hamburg, wir freuen uns, Sie im Hamburger Hafen begrüßen zu dürfen« – die Schiffsbegrüßungsanlage am Schulauer Fährhaus in Wedel, der weltweit bekannte »Welcome Point«, empfängt die Riesen des Ozeans in der jeweiligen Landessprache und mit den Nationalhymnen des Heimatlandes. Der diensthabende »Begrüßungskapitän« kann über 150 Nationalhymnen und Ansagen in mehr als 40 Sprachen seefahrender Nationen einspielen. Zur Begrüßung senkt er die Hamburger Flagge am 40 Meter hohen Mast und das Schiff antwortet ebenfalls mit dem Dippen der Flagge.

"Willkommen in Hamburg. It is our great pleasure to welcome you to the Port of Hamburg" – the ship's tannoy at the Schulauer Fährhaus in Wedel, the world famous "Welcome Point", receives the giants of the sea in their national language while playing their national anthem. The officiating captain manning the welcome station can play more than 150 national anthems and welcome messages in the languages of over 40 seagoing nations. He lowers the Hamburg flag on the 40-metre high mast in welcome, and the incoming ship responds by lowering its flag, too.

Die Schiffsbegrüßungsanlage Willkomm-Höft wurde am 12. Juni 1952 in Betrieb genommen. Auf dem Fähranleger ist eine große Lautsprecheranlage montiert. Jedes größere Schiff, das den Hamburger Hafen anläuft oder wieder verlässt, erhält hier zwischen acht und 20 Uhr einen Willkommens- oder Abschiedsgruß. Bei auslaufenden Schiffen wird zusätzlich zur Hamburger Flagge das Signal UW (= Gute Reise) aufgezogen. Den Gästen des Schulauer Fährhauses vermitteln die Begrüßungskapitäne in der Kommando-zentrale über Lautsprecher vielfältige Informationen über das jeweilige Schiff.

The welcoming station at Höft began operation on 12 June 1952. A large tannoy system is installed on the ferry wharf from which every large ship that sails into or leaves Hamburg Port between 8 a.m. and 8 p.m. receives a welcome or farewell message. Departing ships also receive the signal UW (= bon voyage). The officiating captain provides guests of the Schulauer Fährhaus with a range of different information about each of the ships.

msc
msc
LLOYD TRIESTINO
msc
msc
LOTSE
M

Ein Versetzboot bringt den Lotsen zum Schiff. Zunächst kommt vor Cuxhaven der Seelotse an Bord, dann bei Brunsbüttel an der Einfahrt zum Nord-Ostsee-Kanal der Elblotse und bei Teufelsbrück übernimmt der Hafenlotse bis zum Kai.

A pilot boat brings the pilot to the ship. Just before Cuxhaven, the first pilot comes aboard; then, at Brunsbüttel, at the entryway to the Kiel Canal, the Elbe pilot; and at Teufelsbrück the port pilot takes over to guide the ship to the quay.

Drei Schlepper haben den 332 Meter langen Erzfrachter »Peene Ore« der Reederei F. Laeisz auf den Haken genommen, beim Stapellauf 1997 mit einer Vermessung von 155.051 BRZ (Bruttoraumzahl) das größte Handelsschiff unter deutscher Flagge. Eine generelle Pflicht zur Annahme von Hafenschleppern gibt es in Hamburg nicht. Die meisten Kapitäne großer Seeschiffe nehmen aus Sicherheitsgründen aber ihre Hilfe in Anspruch. Moderne Hafenschlepper sind hoch motorisierte Alleskönner: Sie können seitwärts fahren, auf der Stelle drehen und die Schiffe lenken, schleppen, bugsieren, bremsen und schieben.

The picture shows three tugs pulling the 332 metre-long ore carrier “Peene Ore” owned by shipping company F. Laeisz. At its launch in 1997 it was the largest ship trading under a German flag, measuring 155,051 gross tonnage (‘GT’, registered tonnage). While there is no general obligation to accept harbour tugs in Hamburg, the captains of most large seagoing vessels accept their help for safety reasons. Modern port tugboats are highly-motorised all-rounders: they can sail sideways, turn on the spot and steer, pull, tow, brake and push the ships.

Schlepper von Petersen & Alpers warten an der Schlepperstation Neumühlen auf ihren Einsatz. Die 1793 gegründete Reederei ist der älteste noch im Familienbesitz befindliche Dienstleistungsbetrieb im Hafen und eines von fünf Mitgliedern der Arbeitsgemeinschaft der Seeschiffassistenz-Reedereien. Im Hamburger Hafen stehen etwa 20 Schlepper zur Verfügung. Aus Sicherheitsgründen haben die Schiffe meist den Antrieb vorn und die Schleppwinde hinten. Maßstab der Leistungsfähigkeit ist der tatsächliche Trossenzug (»Pfahlzug«). Moderne Schlepper bieten eine Leistung bis zu 75 Tonnen Pfahlzug.

Petersen & Alpers tugboats wait at the tugboat station Neumühlen until they are needed. This shipping company, founded in 1793, is the oldest service provider in the port that is still a family-run business and one of five members of the Association of Seafaring Vessels Assistance Companies. Around 20 tugboats are available in the Port of Hamburg. In the interests of safety, the ships usually have their motor at the front and the winch at the back. The measure of capacity is the actual bollard pull. Modern tugboats have a capacity of up to 75 tonnes bollard pull.

Jedes Schiff, das den Hamburger Hafen anläuft oder wieder verlässt, ist auf die Hilfe der Festmacher angewiesen. Im Hafen sorgen fünf Unternehmen der Arbeitsgemeinschaft der Hamburger Schiffsbefestiger mit rund 100 Mitarbeitern, 17 Festmacherbooten und 20 »Winschenwagen« dafür, dass die Schiffe rund um die Uhr schnell und sicher vertäut und wieder losgemacht werden. Die Festmacher erwarten das eingehende Schiff bereits an seinem vorgehaltenen Liegeplatz und arbeiten in Abstimmung mit der Schiffsführung entweder von Land oder vom Wasser aus.

Every ship that sails into or out of the Port of Hamburg relies on the assistance of the lines handlers. In the port, five companies from within the Association of Hamburg Mooring Companies with around 100 employees, 17 mooring tugs and 20 winch trolleys ensure that the ships can be quickly and safely tied up and cast off around the clock. The lines handlers await the incoming vessel at its designated berth and work in cooperation with the ship's command either from land or water.

Zwei Mann auf dem Kai stellen über eine Wurfleine die erste Verbindung zum Schiff her. An den Wurfleinen werden die Festmachertrossen vom Bug und vom Heck des Schiffes auf den Kai gezogen und mit dem »Auge« über den Poller gelegt. Anschließend zieht sich das Schiff quer an die Kaimauer heran. Heute arbeiten die Festmacher mit Autos auf dem Kai, auf denen Winden mit einer Zugkraft von bis zu einer Tonne montiert sind. Dennoch müssen Festmacher immer noch ordentlich zupacken können – und wenn eines der armdicken Schiffstaue reißt, wird es für sie höchst gefährlich.

Two men on the quay use a throwline to make the first connection with the ship. Using the throwlines, the mooring lines are pulled to the quay from both bow and stern and wound around the bollard using the "eye". The ship is then pulled in towards the quay sideways. Nowadays, the mooring lines are attached to vehicles on the quay, which are fitted with winches with a bollard pull of up to one tonne. Nevertheless, the lines handlers still need a very strong grip – if one of the ropes (which are as thick as a man's arm) were to give way, the situation could become extremely dangerous.

Die hamburgische Flagge weht am Mast einer HADAG-Fähre. Über 120 große und kleine deutsche Reedereien haben ihren Sitz in der Freien und Hansestadt, darüber hinaus sind hier zahlreiche ausländische Schifffahrtsunternehmen durch Niederlassungen vertreten, wie z.B. die Containerreederei APL Co. (Singapur), oder sie sind an Hamburger Firmen beteiligt wie der weltweit tätige, auf Bananen, Melonen und Ananas spezialisierte irischstämmige Fruchtvermarkter Fyffes. Die Tanker der United Product Tanker (UPT) mit Sitz in Hamburg fahren hauptsächlich im Nordamerikadienst und im Mittelmeer.

The Hamburg flag flies from the mast of a HADAG ferry. More than 120 large and small German shipping companies are based in the Free and Hanseatic City, and numerous overseas shipping companies, such as container ship company APL Co. (Singapore), also have offices here or hold shares in Hamburg companies, like globally active Ireland-based fruit distributor Fyffes, which has specialised in bananas, melons and pineapple. The tankers of Hamburg-based United Product Tanker (UPT) sail mainly the North American route and to the Mediterranean.

Von Hamburg aus werden fast 1500 Schiffe und damit gut die Hälfte der deutschen Handelsflotte bereedert. Gemessen an der Tonnage nimmt Deutschland mit neun Prozent an der Welthandelsflotte den dritten Rang ein. Die Hapag-Lloyd, deren Anfänge auf das Jahr 1847 zurückgehen, und die Hamburg Süd (1871) zählen zu den ältesten deutschen Reedereien; E.R. Schifffahrt führt als maritimer Dienstleister die Schifffahrtstradition der Familie Rickmers fort. Die südkoreanische Hanjin Shipping Co., eine der größten Reedereien der Welt, hat ihre Europazentrale in Hamburg.

Almost 1,500 ships - over half of the German trading fleet - are operated from Hamburg. Measured in terms of tonnage, Germany, with nine percent, takes third place in the world trading fleet. Hapag-Lloyd, which dates back to 1847, and Hamburg Süd (1871) are among the oldest German shipping companies; E.R. Schifffahrt is continuing the seagoing tradition of the Rickmers family as a maritime service provider. The South-Korean Hanjin Shipping Co., one of the largest shipping companies in the world, also has its European headquarters in Hamburg.

CMA CGM

Die 365,5 Meter lange und 51,2 Meter breite »Christophe Colomb« ist das Flaggschiff der französischen Reederei CMA CGM (Marseille). Voll beladen kann der Containerfrachter 13.800 TEU (20-Fuß-Standardcontainereinheiten) transportieren und zählt damit zu den größten Schiffen, die in Hamburg festmachen. Wegen des Tiefgangs der Elbe kann das Schiff allerdings nur etwa 8000 Container in den Hafen bringen. Eine vergleichbare Kapazität hat auch die »Malik Al Ashtar« der in den Golfstaaten beheimateten United Arab Shipping Company (UASC), die am Terminal Burchardkai im Waltershofer Hafen festgemacht hat.

The "Christophe Colomb", measuring 365.5 metres in length and 51.2 metres wide is the flagship of French shipping company CMA CGM (Marseille). Fully loaded, this container ship can transport 13,800 TEU (Twenty Foot Equivalent Unit, equivalent to a 20-foot container unit), making it one of the largest ships to dock in Hamburg. However, due to the restrictions posed by the depth of the Elbe, the ship can transport only around 8,000 containers to the port. The "Malik Al Ashtar", which is owned by United Arab Shipping Company (UASC) based in the Gulf States and which docked at the Burchard Quay in the Waltershof Port, has a similar capacity.

Der Frachter »CMA CGM Quartz« (4360 TEU) wird am Terminal Burchardkai entladen. Für den schnellen Güterumschlag stehen in Hamburg vier große Terminals zur Verfügung: Burchardkai in Waltershof, Tollerort (Neuhof) und Altenwerder betreibt die Hamburger Hafen und Logistik AG (HHLA), den Eurogate Containerterminal (Waltershof) die gleichnamige Unternehmensgruppe. Das 2002 in Betrieb genommene Terminal Altenwerder zählt durch seinen weitestgehend automatisierten Umschlag mit fahrerlosen Transportfahrzeugen zu den weltweit modernsten Umschlaganlagen.

The freighter "CMA CGM Quartz" (4360 TEU) is being unloaded at the Burchard Quay Terminal. Four large terminals are available in Hamburg to facilitate swift transshipment: Burchard Quay in Waltershof, Tollerort (Neuhof) and Altenwerder are all operated by Hamburger Hafen und Logistik AG (HHLA), the Eurogate Container Terminal (Waltershof) by the corporate group of the same name. The Altenwerder Terminal, which began operations in 2002, is one of the most modern transshipment facilities in the world with its largely automated transshipment system and unmanned automatic transport vehicles.

Mit ihrer Höhe von gut 80 Metern und den mächtigen wasserseitigen Auslegern sind die Containerbrücken das neue Wahrzeichen des Hamburger Hafens. Sie haben eine erheblich höhere Umschlagsfrequenz als herkömmliche Kaikräne. Bedient werden sie von einem Brückenfahrer, der von seinem Arbeitsplatz in der schwebenden Kabine unter der Kranbrücke, der »Hauptkatze«, alle Arbeitsschritte steuert und überwacht. Er setzt das Lastaufnahmemittel, den Spreader, auf den Container auf. Sind beide fest miteinander verriegelt, kann der Container angehoben und zu seinem vorgesehenen Platz bewegt werden.

Measuring a good 80 metres and with their impressive outriggers at the waterside the container bridges have become the new landmark of the Port of Hamburg. They have a significantly higher turnover rate than traditional quay cranes and are operated by a crane driver, who controls and supervises all processes from his position in the cabin suspended under the crane bridge. He places the lifting device, the "spreader", on the container. Once both are safely locked together, the container can be lifted and moved to its designated spot.

Auf den meisten speziell für den Containerverkehr eingerichteten Schiffen werden die Boxen in Längsrichtung befördert. Die Laderäume auf fast allen Vollcontainerschiffen sind mit »Cell Guides« ausgestattet. Diese vertikalen Führungsschienen ermöglichen einen schnellen Umschlag und eine sichere Stauung an Bord. Zur Beförderung der Container auf dem Terminal werden Van Carrier eingesetzt – im Hafenjargon nach einem der ersten deutschen Hersteller dieser Portalhubwagen auch Peiner genannt. Moderne Van Carrier bewältigen bis zu 50 Tonnen Hublast und stapeln Container in bis zu vier Lagen.

On the majority of ships equipped specifically for container shipping, the boxes are transported longitudinally. The cargo holds on almost all fully containerised ships are fitted with "cell guides". These vertical guide rails facilitate the swift transshipment and safe storage on board. Van carriers are used at the terminal to transport the containers – these are known locally as "Peiner" after the first German manufacturer of this type of straddle carrier. Modern van carriers have a lifting capacity of up to 50 tonnes and can stack containers in up to four layers.

Container sind nach internationalen Regeln standardisierte Beförderungsbehälter. Ein 20-Fuß-Standardcontainer ist 6,058 Meter (= 20 Fuß) lang, 2,438 Meter breit und 2,591 Meter hoch. Das Gesamtgewicht darf maximal 24.000 Kilogramm betragen. Jeder Container erhält bei seiner Registrierung eine weltweit genormte eindeutige Nummer. Sie besteht aus dem Eigentümer- und dem Produktgruppenschlüssel, der sechsstelligen Registriernummer und einer Prüfziffer. Drehverschlüsse, die »Twistlocks«, dienen zur Sicherung von Containern an Bord.

Transport containers are standardised according to international rules. A 20-foot-standard container is 6.058 metres (= 20 feet) long, 2.438 metres wide and 2.591 metres high. The total weight may not exceed 24,000 kilograms. On registration, each container is allocated a globally standardised number. The number comprises the owner and product-group codes, a six-digit registration number and a check digit. The containers are secured on board using twistlocks.

Blick von den St.-Pauli-Landungsbrücken auf die beiden bekanntesten Museumsschiffe im Hafen: Der Segler »Rickmer Rickmers« wurde im August 1896 in Dienst gestellt. Von Chile kommend geriet das Schiff 1916 in portugiesische Hände. 1983 kam der Windjammer durch private Initiative nach Hamburg und liegt seit September 1987 hier vor Anker. Die Überseebrücke ist seit November 1990 Liegeplatz der »Cap San Diego«. Der 1962 in Dienst gestellte Stückgutfrachter fuhr bis 1981 im Südamerikadienst, wurde dann nach Spanien verkauft und im Herbst 1986 vor der Verschrottung bewahrt.

The view from the St. Pauli Piers to the two best-known museum ships in the port: the sailing ship "Rickmer Rickmers" was launched in August 1896. En route from Chile the ship fell into Portuguese hands in 1916. In 1983, the Windjammer was brought to Hamburg as the result of a private initiative and has been anchored here since September 1987. Since November 1990 the "Cap San Diego" has been berthed at the Überseebrücke (lit. Overseas Bridge). This cargo freighter, which operated on the South America route from 1962 to 1981, was sold to Spain, before being saved from the breaker's yard in autumn 1986.

Als »Bahnhof am Wasser« wurden die St.-Pauli-Landungsbrücken 1909 ihrer Bestimmung übergeben und seither mehrfach umgestaltet. Die Anlage besteht aus Pontons und ist durch neun Brücken mit dem Festland verbunden. Zwischen den Pontons und dem Ufer liegen die Hafenrundfahrtbarkassen. Auf dem Dach des 1966 erbauten ehemaligen Kaispeichers A auf der Landspitze Kaiserhöft entsteht Hamburgs prägnantestes Bauwerk: die Elbphilharmonie. In Sichtweite liegt der Sandtorhafen, zu dessen Traditionsschiffen auch der 1908 gebaute kohlenbefeuerte Dampfer »Schaarhörn« gehört.

The St. Pauli Piers began operation as a "station by the water" in 1909 and have been renovated several times since. The site consists of pontoons with nine bridges connecting it to the mainland. Between the pontoons and the shore are the harbour tour barges. Atop the former quay warehouse A, built in 1966, on the tongue of land known as Kaiserhöft, Hamburg's most impressive building is under construction: the Elbe Philharmonic Hall. It overlooks the Sandtorhafen with its traditional sailing ships, among them the "Schaarhörn", a coal-powered steamer built in 1908.

Die russische Viermastbark »Kruzenshtern« (Länge: 114,5 m, 3400 m² Segelfläche) zählt zu den häufigen Gästen des seit 1977 alljährlich um den 7. Mai herum mit einem Volksfest gefeierten Hafengeburtstages. Das Schiff verkörpert auch ein wichtiges Kapitel hamburgischer Seefahrtsgeschichte: 1926 auf den Namen »Padua« getauft, gehörte der Rahsegler zu den berühmten Flying-P-Linern der Reederei F. Laeisz und diente 1943 als Filmkulisse für »Große Freiheit Nr. 7« mit Hans Albers. 1946 wurde das Schiff an die Sowjetunion übergeben und segelt seither als Schulschiff.

The Russian four-masted barque "Kruzenshtern" (length: 114.5 m, 3400 m² sail area) is one of the most regular guests at the Port birthday celebrations, which have been marked around 7 May every year since 1977 with a fair. The ship also embodies an important chapter in Hamburg's seagoing history: christened the "Padua" at its launch in 1926, the square sailed ship was one of the famous Flying-P-Liners of the shipping company F. Laeisz and in 1943 served as the film set for the film "Große Freiheit Nr. 7" featuring Hans Albers. In 1946, the ship was handed over to the Soviet Union and since then has sailed as a training ship.

Gut anderthalb Millionen Menschen kommen jedes Jahr zum Hafengeburtstag und feiern auf der Hafenmeile zwischen Baumwall und St.-Pauli-Landungsbrücken ein fröhliches Volksfest. Höhepunkte sind die Einlaufparade, für die auch auf der altehrwürdigen »Cap San Diego« die Schiffsdiesel angeworfen werden, und das gut einstündige »Schlepperballett« an den Landungsbrücken, wenn die wendigen PS-Protze in weltweit einzigartiger Schau zu Walzerklängen tanzen. Mit der großen Auslaufparade geht der Hafengeburtstag wieder zu Ende - auf ein Neues im nächsten Jahr.

Around 1.5 million people visit the harbour birthday celebrations every year to celebrate with a funfair on the promenade between Baumwall and the St. Pauli Piers. The highpoints are the parade, for which even the venerable "Cap San Diego" fires up its engines, and the "Schlepperballett" at the piers, when the hugely powerful yet highly manoeuvrable tugs dance to the rhythms of a waltz in a unique hour-long show. The huge closing parade marks the end of the birthday celebrations - until the next year.

Drei Kreuzfahrtanleger gibt es an der Norderelbe: in der HafenCity, an der Überseebrücke und in Altona. Die »MSC Magnifica«, die im März 2010 in Hamburg von Sophia Loren getauft wurde, ist regelmäßig zu Gast. Hamburg ist eine beliebte Kreuzfahrtdestination – übrigens wurde diese Art des Reisens auch hier erfunden: Da seine Luxusliner auf der Nordamerika-Route im Winter nicht ausgelastet waren, schickte der damalige Hapag-Chef Albert Ballin am 22. Januar 1891 den Schnelldampfer »Auguste Viktoria« auf eine zweimonatige Vergnügungstour durch das Mittelmeer.

There are three cruise ship berths on the North Elbe: in HafenCity, at the Überseebrücke and in Altona. The "MSC Magnifica", which was christened by Sophia Loren in March 2010, is a regular guest. Hamburg is one of the most popular cruise destinations – indeed, this form of travel was invented here! Because his luxury liners were not used to full capacity on the North American Route during the winter months, Albert Ballin, the boss of Hapag at that time, first sent the steamship the "Auguste Viktoria" on a pleasure tour of the Mediterranean on 22 January 1891.

Events wie die seit 2008 alle zwei Jahre im Hafen stattfindenden Hamburg Cruise Days und spektakuläre Schiffstaufen wie die des Kreuzfahrtschiffs »AIDAmar« während des 823. Hafengeburtstages am 12. Mai 2012 locken Hunderttausende. Zu den immer wieder gern gesehenen Gästen zählt auch die 345 Meter lange »Queen Mary 2«, bei ihrer Indienststellung 2003 das größte Kreuzfahrtschiff der Welt (148.528 BRZ). Sie kann 2620 Passagiere höchst luxuriös über die Weltmeere schippern. Deutlich bescheidener kommt die »MS Columbus 2« daher, die maximal 698 Gästen Platz bietet.

Events like the biennial Hamburg Cruise Days, which have been held at the Port since 2008, and spectacular launch ceremonies like that for the cruise ship "AIDAmar" during the 823rd harbour birthday celebrations on 12 May 2012, draw thousands of visitors. Among the most welcome and frequent guests is the 345-metre long "Queen Mary 2", which at its commissioning in 2003 was the largest cruise ship in the world (148,528 GT). It can transport 2,620 passengers across the world's oceans in the most luxurious of settings. The "MS Columbus 2" is much more modest, with a maximum capacity of 698 guests.

Jeden Sonntag ab fünf Uhr (im Winter ab sieben Uhr) zieht der Fischmarkt Zehntausende an den Hafenrand. An den Verkaufsständen unter freiem Himmel auf der Großen Elbstraße wird mit fast allem gehandelt, was sich an das buntgestaltige Publikum bringen lässt: Touristen und Einheimische, Frühaufsteher und Nachtschwärmer erfreuen sich an der Originalität des Marktgeschehens und am marktschreierischen Einfallsreichtum der Verkäufer. Zum stilvollen Brunch lädt die Fischauktionshalle ein, 1895/96 von der damals noch selbstständigen Stadt Altona errichtet.

Every Sunday from 5 a.m. (7 a.m. in winter) the fish market attracts tens of thousands of visitors to the edge of the port. Outdoor stalls on the Große Elbstraße sell practically everything under the sun to the colourful crowd: tourists and locals, early birds and night owls alike enjoy the uniqueness of the bustling market and the inventiveness of the stallholders touting their wares. The fish auction hall, built in 1895/96 by the town of Altona, which at that time was still separate from Hamburg, is the perfect place to head for a stylish brunch.

Ein paar Kilometer elbabwärts verlockt die »Strandperle« zu einem Besuch. Direkt am Strand von Oevelgönne gelegen, ist dieser traditionsreiche, schon seit 1973 bestehende Selbstbedienungskiosk mit seiner umfangreichen Getränkekarte ein Treffpunkt für Junge und Junggebliebene. Klaglos reihen sich die Gäste in die scheinbar stets gleich langen Schlangen vor der Ausgabe ein und nehmen dann auf einem der wenigen Stühle oder im Sand Platz – die Atmosphäre ist urig und die Aussicht auf die in nächster Nähe vorbeifahrenden Ozeanriesen sorgt gratis für eine deftige Portion Fernweh.

A few kilometres downstream, the "Strandperle" also receives many visitors. Situated directly on the beach at Oevelgönne, this self-service kiosk, steeped in tradition and in business since 1973 with its extensive drinks menu, is a popular meeting place for the young – and the young-at-heart. Without complaint, the guests queue at the counter in a line that seems never to get any shorter, before taking a seat on one of the few chairs or on the sand. The atmosphere is relaxed and the views of the giant ocean liners passing at close quarters provide a hearty portion of wanderlust, free of charge.

Von den St.-Pauli-Landungsbrücken starten nicht nur die HADAG-Hafenfähren im Hamburger Verkehrsverbund, sondern auch die Hafenrundfahrten. Die »Kurt Abicht« der Reederei Rainer Abicht gehört zu den »klassischen« Barkassen: Das 1943 gebaute Schiff von 18,70 Metern Länge und einem Tiefgang von 1,65 Metern diente ursprünglich zum »Leute versetzen«, also zur Beförderung von jeweils gut 100 Hafenarbeitern zu ihren Arbeitsplätzen und ihrer Rückfahrt zu den Landungsbrücken. Heute genießen an Bord der »Kurt Abicht« bis zu 70 Passagiere das Erlebnis einer Hafenrundfahrt.

Both the HADAG harbour ferries which form part of Hamburg's public transport network, and the harbour tours set out from the St. Pauli Piers. The "Kurt Abicht", owned by shipping company Rainer Abicht, is one of the "traditional" barges: the vessel, measuring 18.70 metres in length, was built in 1943 and with a draught of 1.65 metres originally served to move people, that is, to transport around 100 harbour workers between their workplaces and the piers. Today, up to 70 passengers can enjoy an exciting harbour tour aboard the "Kurt Abicht".

Die »Ursula Glitscher« (Baujahr: 1921) in voller Fahrt auf der Elbe. Der touristische Aspekt des Hamburger Hafens wurde schon im letzten Jahrhundert entdeckt. Am 1. Juli 1921 übertrug die Stadt der Fährschiffsreederei HADAG das Privileg für die »Große Hafenrundfahrt«. Mit diesem jahrzehntelang geltenden Monopol sollte auch der Service deutlich verbessert werden: Nicht selten quittierten die Hafen- und Werftarbeiter die wortreichen Ausführungen der »Hafenerklärer« mit einem laut vernehmlichen »He lücht« (Er lügt), was mittlerweile ihre inoffizielle Berufsbezeichnung ist.

The "Ursula Glitscher" (built in 1921) at full tilt on the Elbe. The tourist aspect of the Port of Hamburg was discovered in the last century. On 1 July 1921 the city granted the ferry shipping company HADAG the privilege to operate the "large harbour tour". This monopoly, which spanned several decades, was also hoped to result in improvements to the service. However, the harbour and wharf workers frequently commented on the verbose explanations of the guides with a clearly audible "He lücht" (he's lying), which has come in the meantime to be used as the unofficial job title.

BLOHM+VOSS DOCK 10
ThyssenKrupp
Marine Systems

AUMUND

Der ehrenamtlich geführte Museumshafen Oevelgönne bewahrt seit Mai 1977 die Erinnerung an die Segel- und Dampfschifffahrt auf der Niederelbe sowie im Nord- und Ostseeraum. Ein Feuerschiff ist hier vertäut, auch Elb-Ewer, Dampfschlepper, Segelschiffe, Barkassen und Boote von Polizei und Zoll. Die meisten dieser Arbeitsschiffe stammen aus der Zeit zwischen 1880 und 1930. Links das einstige Union-Kühlhaus, 1924 für Gefrierfleisch errichtet und 1993 zum Wohnstift Augustinum umgebaut. Solvente Senioren erfüllen sich hier den Traum vom Alterssitz mit Elbblick.

Since May 1977, the Museum Port of Oevelgönne, run on a voluntary basis, has been keeping alive the memories of the age of sailing and steamships on the lower Elbe, North Sea and Baltic Sea regions. A lightship is moored here, as are Elbe-scullers, steam-tugs, sailing ships, barges, police and customs boats. Most of these working ships date from between 1880 and 1930. To the left, the former Union Refrigerated Warehouse, built in 1924 to store meat and transformed into a retirement home in 1993. Here, wealthy pensioners can live out their dreams of a home with views of the Elbe.

Historische Kaikräne, der 1958 gebaute Stückgutfrachter »MS Bleichen« und der Schwimmkran »Saatsee« von 1917 gehören zu den größten Ausstellungsstücken des Hafenmuseums im historischen Schuppen 50 am Bremer Kai im Hansahafen. In jahrzehntelanger Arbeit wurde eine einzigartige Sammlung zusammengetragen und gibt Einblick in den Hafenumschlag vor dem Siegeszug des Containers – an einem historischen Ort, Hamburgs letztem Kaischuppen aus der Kaiserzeit. Noch in den 1980er Jahren wurden in den »50er-Schuppen« die Ladungen ungezählter Seeschiffe aus aller Welt umgeschlagen.

Historic quay cranes, the cargo freighter the "MS Bleichen", built in 1958, and the floating crane the "Saatsee" dating from 1917 are among the largest exhibits of the Harbour Museum in the historic transit shed 50 on the Bremer Quay in the Hansa Port. Over several decades, a unique collection has been put together here in a historic setting, Hamburg's last quayside transit shed dating from the time of the Kaiser. The museum provides an insight into harbour transit prior to the triumphant advance of the container. Until the 1980s, the cargo of countless ships from all around the world was transhipped here.

COSCO
COSCO HELLAS

Eine Hafenrundfahrt führt bei Hochwasser natürlich auch durch die Speicherstadt, den größten zusammenhängenden Lagerhauskomplex der Welt. Bei einer Barkassenfahrt in den langgezogenen Fleeten zwischen den Gebäudereihen lässt sich auch die zweckmäßige Architektur studieren: Die unbeheizten Lagerböden ermöglichten gute klimatische Lagerbedingungen für Kaffee, Tee und Gewürze, die Speichergebäude entsprachen dem zu ihrer Bauzeit neuesten Stand der Technik, sie verfügten über elektrisches Licht und über am Hausgiebel montierte hydraulisch betriebene Winden.

A tour of the harbour at high tide of course also includes the Speicherstadt, the largest interconnected warehouse complex in the world. A barge trip along the long, narrow fleets between the rows of buildings provides a unique opportunity to study the functional architecture: the unheated warehouse flooring allowed for good climactic storage conditions for coffee, tea and spices. At the time of construction, the warehouses were state-of-the art, with electric lighting and hydraulic winches mounted at the gable.

Die Speicherstadt war jahrzehntelang das Domizil der Quartiersleute, die sich um die Einlagerung sowie die Kontrolle und Pflege, Bearbeitung und Veredelung von Gütern kümmern. Die Bezeichnung kommt daher, dass die Firmengründung meist zu viert (lateinisch quattuor = vier) erfolgte. Namensgeber war der Vormann, die Teilhaber erschienen als »& Consorten«. Mittlerweile sind viele Traditionsfirmen aus der Speicherstadt in andere Hafenteile umgezogen, wie die auf Gewürze und Trockenfrüchte spezialisierte Fa. Werner Bruhns und die Fa. Wolter Lagerhaus, Experte für Trocken- und Hülsenfrüchte.

For many decades, the Speicherstadt was the home of the quartermasters, who oversaw the storage, supervision, care, processing and refinement of the goods. Their title is based on the fact that companies were usually established by four parties (Latin quattuor = four). The company was named after the foreman, the shareholders appeared as “& Consorts”. In the meantime, many long-established companies, such as spice and dried fruits specialists Werner Bruhns, and Wolter Lagerhaus, experts for dried fruit and pulses, have relocated from the Speicherstadt to other parts of the harbour area.

Blick auf die von sechs Fleeten durchzogene Speicherstadt, rechts am nördlichen Rand verläuft der Zollkanal. Er schuf unter Umgehung des 1888 errichteten Freihafens eine freie Durchfahrt für Binnenschiffe und bildet seit Errichtung des Stadtteils HafenCity die Abgrenzung zur Altstadt. Die Speicherstadt entstand zwischen 1885 und 1927 in drei großen Bauabschnitten und umfasste bei ihrer Fertigstellung 24 Speicherblöcke mit rund 310.000 Quadratmetern Lagerfläche. Heute beherbergen die Speicher u.a. Büros, Tee- und Teppichhändler, mehrere Museen sowie Unterhaltungsangebote wie das Miniatur Wunderland.

View of the Speicherstadt, dissected by six fleets. To the right, on the northern edge runs the customs channel. Circumventing the free port created in 1888, it created a free passage for inland ships and, since the creation of the HafenCity area, has formed the boundary to the Old Town. The Speicherstadt was built between 1885 and 1927 in three large construction phases and on completion comprised 24 warehouse blocks with a storage area of around 310,000 square metres. Today, the warehouses are home to offices, tea and carpet traders among others, as well as several museums and entertainment venues, such as "miniature wonderland".

Blick über das »Portugiesenviertel« zwischen Baumwall und Landungsbrücken auf die Norderelbe und Steinwerder mit den mächtigen Docks von Blohm + Voss. Dahinter erstrecken sich die Umschlagsanlagen der großen Containerterminals. Tag und Nacht sind die Containerbrücken in Bewegung, beladen oder löschen die an der Wasserseite liegenden Schiffe und holen oder setzen mit schlafwandlerischer Sicherheit die Container auf der Landseite ab, wo sie von Portalhubwagen oder – beim Terminal Altenwerder – von automatisierten Fahrzeugen gebracht oder geholt werden.

View overlooking the "Portuguese Quarter" between Baumwall and the Landing Piers on the Norderelbe and Steinwerder, with the imposing docks of Blohm + Voss. The transhipment facilities of the huge container terminals stretch out in the background. The container bridges are in motion day and night, loading or unloading the ships and collecting or placing the containers with absolute precision on the quayside where they are brought or collected by straddle carriers or – at the Altenwerder Terminal – by automated vehicles.

Mit einer Barkasse geht es bei der Großen Hafenrundfahrt auch vorbei an Blohm + Voss, wo gerade der 229 Meter lange japanische Massengutfrachter »Eden Maru« (Tragfähigkeit: 63.636 tdw = tonnes dead weight) einer Generalüberholung im Trockendock unterzogen wird. Es ist immer wieder ein imposanter Anblick, die Riesen der Meere einmal aus der Nähe in ganzer Größe zu sehen. Im Dock werden alle Arbeiten vorgenommen, die sonst nicht möglich sind, wie die Ausbesserung von Schäden und die Erneuerung des Unterwasseranstrichs, um durch geringere Reibungsverluste Treibstoff einzusparen.

During a full tour of the harbour, the barge also sails past Blohm + Voss, where the picture shows 229-metre-long Japanese bulk cargo carrier "Eden Maru" (load capacity: 63,636 tdw = tonnes dead weight) undergoing a general overhaul in the dry dock. It is always an impressive sight to see the full enormity of these ocean giants at close quarters. All of the tasks that are not otherwise possible are carried out in the dock, such as repairs and renewing the underwater paint, which helps save fuel by reducing the frictional loss.

Nur bei einer Hafenrundfahrt kommt man ganz nahe an die Ozeanriesen heran und erlebt hautnah die Faszination von Fernweh, Freiheit und Abenteuer, die das stets pulsierende Hafenleben ausstrahlt. Mit ein wenig Glück lassen sich in dem Gewimmel von Schiffen und Booten unterschiedlichster Art und Größe auch spektakuläre Neubauten entdecken wie die auf der Werft Blohm + Voss für den russischen Milliardär Roman Abramowitsch gebaute und mit allen nur denkbaren Annehmlichkeiten ausgestattete »Eclipse«, mit 162,5 Metern die längste Megayacht der Welt.

Only on a tour of the harbour can one get this close to these giants of the sea to experience at first hand the fascination of wanderlust, freedom and adventure that harbour life exudes. With a bit of luck, visitors can admire models of the most diverse types and sizes among the many ships and boats, including spectacular new-builds like the "Eclipse", built at the Blohm + Voss wharf for Russian millionaire Roman Abramovich, which features every conceivable comfort, and, at 162.5 metres, is the longest mega-yacht in the world.

Blick auf die Werft Blohm + Voss. Im Jahr 1877 gegründet, liefen hier viele Ozeanriesen vom Stapel, so z.B. im April 1913 die »Vaterland«, mit 54.282 Bruttoregistertonnen damals das größte Schiff der Welt. Fünf große Docks stehen hier bereit, darunter Elbe 17 - für Schiffe bis 320.000 tdw und mit 352 Metern Länge eines der größten Trockendocks in Europa - und die Schwimmdocks 10 und 11 für Schiffe mit einer Tragfähigkeit von 130.000 bzw. 250.000 tdw. Sie sind aufgrund ihrer Lage gegenüber den Landungsbrücken imposante Blickfänge.

View of the Blohm + Voss wharf. Established in 1877, many ocean giants were built here, like the “Vaterland” which in April 1913 was the world’s largest ship with 54,282 gross registered tonnes. There are five large docks here, including Elbe 17 - for ships with up to 320,000 tdw. At 352 metres long, it is one of the largest dry docks in Europe - and the floating docks 10 and 11 for ships with a load capacity of 130,000 and 250,000 tdw respectively. Positioned directly opposite the Landing Piers, these are impressively eye-catching.

Blohm + Voss ist die letzte Großwerft im Hafen und befasst sich heute vor allem mit Reparaturen und Umbauten. Hamburgs Schiffbau hat eine lange Tradition, die Werften und die damit verbundene Geräuschkulisse prägten jahrzehntelang die Atmosphäre. Außer Blohm + Voss haben auch einige kleinere Werften alle Krisen und Fusionen überstanden und behaupten sich mit dem Bau von Spezialschiffen, Großyachten und Marineschiffen gegen die Konkurrenz aus Asien. Dort werden herkömmliche Containerfrachter längst schneller und billiger gebaut als in Deutschland.

Blohm + Voss is the last large-scale wharf in the port. Today, it deals primarily with repairs and renovations. Hamburg's shipbuilding industry has a long tradition and the wharves and the noise level associated with them dominated the character of the entire area for many decades. Several smaller wharves also survived the crises and mergers and are now making their mark with specialised ships, large yachts and naval ships, despite growing competition from Asia, where standard container freighters can be built faster and more cheaply than in Germany.

Der Hansaport am Sandauhafen ist mit einer Freifläche von 350.000 Quadratmetern Deutschlands größtes Seehafenterminal für Schüttgüter, vor allem Eisenerz und Kohle. Gut 100.000 Tonnen können hier täglich computergesteuert mit vier Löschbrücken aus den mächtigen Laderäumen der Massengutfrachter - auch Bulk Carrier oder einfach Bulker genannt - gelöscht, über einen eigenen Bahnhof mit 15 Gleisen abgefertigt oder auf den großen Freiflächen zur Weiterverladung zwischengelagert werden. Bei einer Kailänge von 760 Metern stehen hier vier Liegeplätze für Seeschiffe zur Verfügung, an weiteren zwei Liegeplätzen können Küstenmotor- und Binnenschiffe anlegen.

The Hansa Port at Sandauhafen is Germany's largest sea port terminal for bulk materials - mainly iron ore and coal - with a 350,000 m^2 temporary storage area. The terminal has a throughput of around 100,000 tonnes every day. Cargo is unloaded from the massive holds of the bulk cargo carriers (also known as bulk carriers or simply 'bulkers') using computer-controlled machinery with four unloading piers. It is then readied for onward travel at a dedicated railway station with 15 platforms, or stored temporarily for subsequent reloading. With a 760-metre long quay, the terminal has four berths for oceangoing ships, with two more for coasters and inland waterway vessels.

NYK LINE

Autoverladung am O'Swaldkai: Mächtige Autotransporter (Car Carrier) der japanischen NYK Line nehmen am Amerikahöft Nutzfahrzeuge und Neu- und Gebrauchtfahrzeuge an Bord. Das 800.000 Quadratmeter große Terminal ist die größte auf rollende Verladungen spezialisierte Anlage im Hamburger Hafen. Beim RoRo-Verkehr (Roll-on/Roll-off) wird die Ladung über landseitige und/oder bordeigene Rampen durch Bug-, Seiten- oder Heckpforten aus eigener Kraft oder durch Zugmaschinen direkt an und von Bord gerollt. Große RoRo-Schiffe haben mehrere höhenverstellbare Decks, die zumeist nicht unterteilt sind und über die ganze Länge des Schiffes laufen.

Vehicle loading at the O'Swald Quay: imposing car-carriers from the Japanese NYK Line loading commercial vehicles, new and used vehicles at Amerikahöft. The terminal, with an area of 800,000 m^2, is the largest facility in the Hamburg Port specialised in rolling loads. In roll-on/roll-off loading, goods are rolled on their own steam or using tractor units onto and off the ship via ramps from the quay and/or the ship itself through doors at the bow, the sides or the stern. Large 'RoRo' ships have several height-adjustable decks, which are not usually subdivided, and run the entire length of the ship.

An der Löschanlage im Kattwykhafen auf der Elbinsel Wilhelmsburg hat der Doppelhüllentanker »Helga Spirit« (115.514 tdw) festgemacht. Der Mineralölkonzern Shell unterhält hier zwei Liegeplätze, die über Rohrleitungen mit der Raffinerie Hamburg-Harburg verbunden sind, wo jährlich etwa 5,5 Millionen Tonnen Rohöl verarbeitet werden können. Neben Shell sind im Hamburger Hafen weitere Firmen mit dem Umschlag, der sicheren Lagerung und der Verarbeitung von Rohöl und Mineralölprodukten beschäftigt. Als Distributionszentrum hat Hamburg für den Mineralölsektor bundesweite Bedeutung.

The double-hulled tanker the "Helga Spirit" (115,514 tdw) has moored at the unloading station in the Kattwykhafen on the Elbe Island of Wilhelmsburg. Oil company Shell has two berths here, which are linked by pipelines with the Hamburg-Harburg refinery, where around 5.5 million tonnes of crude oil are processed each year. In addition to Shell, other companies also tranship, securely store and process crude oil and mineral oil products in the Port of Hamburg. As a distribution centre, Hamburg is of nationwide importance for the mineral oil sector.

Wasserseitiger Umschlag im Getreide Terminal Hamburg (G.T.H.). Das Terminal am Reiherstieg verfügt über eine Lagerkapazität von insgesamt rund 255.000 Tonnen, davon etwa zwei Drittel für Getreide und Ölsaaten. Es gibt einen Liegeplatz für Schiffe bis zu 270 Meter und drei für Binnen- und Küstenmotorschiffe. Futtermittel, Getreide und Ölfrüchte zählen zu den Sauggütern, die mit Saughebern und Greifern aus den Massengutfrachtern gelöscht, umgeladen oder zwischengelagert werden. Mit gut einer Million Tonnen Silokapazität nimmt Hamburg in Europa einen Spitzenplatz ein.

Transshipment on the waterside at the Grain Terminal Hamburg (G.T.H.). The terminal on the Reiherstieg river has a storage capacity of around 255,000 tonnes in total, of which around two-thirds are for cereals and oilseeds. There is a berth for ships of up to 270 metres, as well as three for inland vessels and motorised coastal ships. Fodder, grain and oilseeds are among the suction cargos unloaded from the bulk cargo carriers, reloaded or temporarily stored using siphons and bucket elevators. With a silo capacity of around a million tones, Hamburg is one of the front-runners in Europe.

Das Motorschiff »Shir Khan« nimmt am Liegeplatz Athabaskakai des HHLA Containerterminals Burchardkai seine Ladung auf. Das 85 Meter lange Binnenschiff befördert mit zehn bis zwölf Stundenkilometern bis zu 54 Standardcontainer von Hamburg zum Westhafen in Berlin und umgekehrt. Das Schiff passiert dabei Elbe, Mittellandkanal, Havel und Spree, wofür angesichts der Schiffsbreite von elf Metern dafür an manchen Stellen Maßarbeit nötig ist. Der Transport auf dem Binnenschiff ist deutlich langsamer als auf der Schiene oder der Straße, dafür aber preisgünstiger und umweltfreundlicher.

The motor ship "Shir Khan" is being loaded at its berth, the Athabaska Quay of HHLA Container Terminal Burchard Quay. The 85-metre-long river barge transports up to 54 standard containers from Hamburg to Westhafen in Berlin and back at a speed of ten to twelve kilometres per hour. On its journey, the ship passes through the Elbe, the Mittelland Canal, the Havel and the Spree, in places demanding precision manoeuvring on account of the ship's breadth of eleven metres. While transport by barge is considerably slower than by rail or road, it is less expensive and better for the environment.

Das Binnenschiff »Planeten Tor« passiert einkommend die Lotsenstation Bubendeyufer. Hamburg ist hinter Duisburg und Köln der drittgrößte Binnenhafen, gut 10.000 Binnenschiffe machen jedes Jahr an den rund 100 für sie bestimmten Liegeplätzen fest. Befördert werden vor allem Massengüter. Zwar hat der Hafen über den Elbe-Lübeck-Kanal und den Elbe-Seitenkanal Zugang zur Ostsee und zu den Wasserstraßen in West- und Mitteldeutschland, doch ausgerechnet auf der Elbe fehlt es in vielen Regionen Ostdeutschlands noch an stabilen Fahrwasserverhältnissen.

The barge "Planeten Tor" passes the pilot station Bubendeyufer on its way to the port. Hamburg is the third-largest inland port after Duisburg and Cologne, with around 10,000 river barges mooring at the 100 designated berths every year. It is mainly bulk goods that are transported using this method. While the port has access to the Baltic Sea and the waterways of Central and West German via the Elbe-Lübeck-Canal and the Elbe-Side Canal, there is still a lack of suitable waterway conditions on the Elbe in many regions of East Germany.

Das niederländische Containerschiff »Perceiver« passiert den Süllberg im Stadtteil Blankenese. Mit einer maximalen Beförderungskapazität von 538 TEU (Twenty Foot Equivalent Unit, entspricht einer 20 Fuß Containereinheit) gehört der 117 Meter lange Frachter in die Klasse der »Feederschiffe« (von englisch: to feed = versorgen). Die großen Containerschiffe, die Hamburg anlaufen und ihre Ladung löschen, haben eine Stellplatzkapazität von über 10.000 TEU. Die Feederschiffe mit Kapazitäten von 300 bis mittlerweile gut 1700 TEU dienen zur Weiterverteilung auf kleinere Häfen.

The Dutch container ship "Perceiver" passes the Süllberg in the Blankenese district. With a maximum load capacity of 538 TEU, the 117-metre-long freighter is classed as a "feeder ship". These large container ships, which come to Hamburg to unload, have a stowage capacity of over 10,000 TEU. Nowadays, feeder ships with capacities of 300 to around 1700 TEU are used for onward distribution to smaller ports.

Das Feederschiff »Merwedijk« der dänischen Reederei Unifeeder kann bis zu 705 TEU befördern. Aufgrund seiner Nähe zum Nord-Ostsee-Kanal ist Hamburg im Wettbewerb mit den weiter westlich gelegenen europäischen Seehäfen im Vorteil. Hamburg ist mit über 150 Abfahrten pro Woche der mit Abstand wichtigste Umschlagplatz für den Ostseeraum und Skandinavien - scherzhaft wird Hamburg deshalb auch der »westlichste Ostseehafen« genannt. Gut 50 Feeder-Dienste bedienen von hier aus kleinere Häfen an Nord- und Ostsee bis hin nach Russland.

The feeder ship "Merwedijk", owned by Danish shipping company Unifeeder, can transport up to 705 TEU. Based on its proximity to the Kiel Canal, Hamburg has a competitive advantage over the European seaports located further west. With more than 150 departures a week, Hamburg is by far the most important transhipment hub for the Baltic Sea region and Scandinavia - which is why Hamburg is sometimes jokingly referred to as the "western Baltic Sea Port". From here, around 50 feeder-services serve smaller ports in the North Sea and the Baltic, all the way to Russia.

Die Freibordmarke - nach ihrem Initiator, dem Briten Samuel Plimsoll (1824-98), auch Plimsollmarke genannt - besteht aus einem Ring und einem waagerechten Strich. Seit 1890 soll sie Schiffsverluste als Folge von Überladung verhindern und markiert den höchstzulässigen Tiefgang in verschiedenen jahreszeitlichen Fahrtzonen: TF = Tropen-Frischwasser-Lademarke, F = Frischwasser-Lademarke im Sommer, T = Tropenlademarke, S = Sommerlademarke, W = Winterlademarke, WNA = Winterlademarke im Nordatlantik.

The load line - also called the Plimsoll line after its initiator, the Englishman Samuel Plimsoll (1824-98) - consists of a ring and a horizontal line. It has been used since 1890 to prevent the loss of ships as a result of overloading and marks the highest permissible draught in various seasonal travel zones: TF = tropical freshwater loading mark, F = freshwater loading mark in summer, T = tropical loading mark, S = summer loading mark, W = winter loading mark, WNA = winter loading mark in the North Atlantic.

Ahmings (auf Englisch draught marks) heißen die Tiefgangsmarken am Bug und am Heck eines Seeschiffs zum Ablesen der Eintauchtiefe bzw. der Trimmlage, wobei die »ideelle« Verlängerungslinie der Unterkante des Kiels den Bezugspunkt darstellt. Bei Seeschiffen wird der Tiefgang in Dezimetern oder englischen Fuß angegeben und im metrischen Maß arabisch und im Fußmaß römisch beziffert. Im Wettbewerb Hamburgs mit Rotterdam und anderen Nordseehäfen spielt der - tideabhängige - Tiefgang der Elbe eine wichtige Rolle.

Draught marks is the name given to the marks on the bow and stern of an oceangoing vessel used to show immersion depth and trim, whereby the ideal extension line of the lower edge of the keel is the reference point. The draught depth is stated in decimetres or English feet; metric is stated in Arabic, feet in Roman numerals. The tide-dependent depth of the Elbe plays an important role in Hamburg's competition with Rotterdam and the other North Sea ports.

Während der Containerumschlag teilweise schon automatisiert verläuft, muss auf einem der Mehrzweckterminals (Multi-Purpose-Terminals) wie dem Buss Hansa Terminal am Stahmerkai im Oderhafen auch immer noch kräftig angepackt werden. Hier werden Schwergut, konventionelles Stückgut (z.B. Fahrzeuge, Maschinen und Industrieanlagen, Forstprodukte, Eisen und Stahl und Südfrüchte) und »Projektladung« umgeschlagen, also Güter, die besonders groß oder sperrig sind und deshalb nicht in einen Container hineinpassen. Dafür braucht es besonderes Equipment und viel Erfahrung.

While container transshipment is partially automated, work at one of the multi-purpose-terminals, like the Buss Hansa Terminal at the Stahmer Quay in Oderhafen, still involves heavy lifting. Bulk cargo, conventional cargo (e.g. vehicles, machinery and industrial equipment, forestry products, iron, steel and tropical fruits) and "project cargo" is transshipped here - i.e. goods that are particularly large or bulky, and will not fit in containers. This demands special equipment and a great deal of experience.

Bis in die 1960er Jahre war die Arbeit am Kai noch harte Handarbeit. Tausende von Arbeitern mit Sackkarre und Muskelkraft holten die Ladung vom Schiff. Im Zuge der Containerisierung hat sich dies geändert. So wurde aus der Tätigkeit des Tallymanns bzw. Quartiersmanns die Fachkraft für Hafenlogistik, aus dem Kaiarbeiter der Hafenfacharbeiter und das Berufsbild der Schauerleute, die im Laderaum unter der Aufsicht eines »Lukenvizen« die Belade- oder Löscharbeiten erledigten, hat sich zur Fachkraft für Lagerlogistik bzw. zum Containerpacker gewandelt.

Until the 1960s, work at the quay still entailed hard manual labour. Thousands of workers used sack barrows and muscle power to unload the ship. This all changed with the advance of containerisation. And the Tallyman or Quartermaster became the harbour logistics specialist; the dockworker became the specialist port worker; and the stevedores, who loaded or unloaded ships under the watchful eye of a “hatch watchman”, are now specialists for warehouse logistics or container packers.

Hamburg hat etwa 2500 Brücken, mehr als jede andere europäische Großstadt. Die Köhlbrandbrücke dominiert seit ihrer Einweihung mit einem großen Volksfest am 20. September 1974 das Hafenpanorama. Die stählerne Schrägseilbrücke hängt mit 88 Trägerseilen an zwei 135 Meter hohen Pylonen. Sie überquert den 325 Meter breiten Köhlbrand, den Mündungsarm der Süder- in die Norderelbe, und verbindet die Stadtteile Steinwerder - mit Blohm + Voss und dem Containerterminal Tollerort - und Waltershof.

Hamburg has around 2,500 bridges - more than any other European city. Since its inauguration with a huge fair on 20 September 1974, the Köhlbrandbrücke has dominated the harbour panorama. The steel cable-stayed bridge is suspended from two 135 metre-high pylons with 88 supports. It spans the 325-metre-wide Köhlbrand, the estuary of the Süder- into the Norderelbe, and links the Steinwerder district - with Blohm + Voss and the container Tollerort Terminal - with Waltershof.

Auf der Waltershofer Seite der Köhlbrandbrücke liegen der Hansaport und die großen Containerterminals Burchardkai, Eurogate sowie Altenwerder. Mit täglich mehr als 30.000 Fahrzeugen ist die Köhlbrandbrücke die wichtigste Verkehrsader des Hafens. Doch die Dauerbelastung durch die immer schwereren Lastwagen machen der Stahlbetonkonstruktion zu schaffen und mit einer lichten Höhe von 54 Metern ist die Brücke zwar heute noch auch von den dicksten Pötten befahrbar, für die künftigen Generationen riesiger Containerschiffe aber wird sie wohl zu niedrig sein.

On the Waltershof side of the Köhlbrandbrücke lie the Hansa Port and the large container terminals Burchard Quay, Eurogate and Altenwerder. With more than 30,000 vehicles crossing every day, the Köhlbrand Bridge is the most important transport route in the port. However, the long-term stress caused by the trucks carrying increasingly heavy loads, is putting pressure on the reinforced concrete structure, and while, with a clearance height of 54 metres, the largest of the big ships can still pass under the bridge, it is likely to be too low for the new generation of giant container ships.

Der unter Singapur-Flagge laufende Massengutfrachter »Stella Anita« (Tragfähigkeit: 180.355 tdw) passiert den Anleger Wittenbergen. Die Arbeitsbedingungen an Bord eines solch modernen Bulk Carriers haben mit der oft besungenen Seemannsromantik früherer Tage nichts zu tun, dem Zuschauer an Land aber mag der Refrain eines Liedes des unvergessenen Hans Albers in den Sinn kommen: »Einmal noch nach Bombay, oder nach Shanghai. Einmal noch nach Rio, oder nach Hawaii. Einmal durch den Suez und durch den Panama! Wieder nach St. Pauli – Hamburg Altona!«

Bulk cargo carrier the "Stella Anita" (load capacity: 180,355 tdw), which sails under a Singapore flag, passing the Wittenbergen pier. The working conditions aboard a modern bulk carrier like this are a far cry from the romantic life described in the old sailor's songs, but spectators on land may yet be reminded of the chorus of a song by the unforgettable Hans Albers: "Back to Bombay or Shanghai, just one more time. Once more to Rio, or maybe to Hawaii. Through the Suez one more time and down the Panama! Then it's back to St. Pauli – to Hamburg Altona!"

© Tide Verlag Zimmermann
Zimmermann-Blum GBR
Karoxbosteler Weg 21 • 21218 Seevetal
Tel. 0 41 05 / 5 40 59 • Fax 63 63 04
Email: tide-verlag@web.de
info@tide-verlag
Tide Verlag
250 m
500 m
750 m
1 km
1,5 km
0
2 km
Alte Süderelbe
Mühlensand
Schilfort
Metha
Süderelbe
Hintzenort
Francoper Außendeich
Francop
Achtern Brack
Vierzigstücken
Hohenwischer Str.
Zur Graft
Brakenburg
Hinterdeich
Hohenwisch
Domsand
Moorburger Elbdeich
Alte Süderelbe
Spleete
Francoper-
Hinterdeich
Moorwettern
Parallelgraben
Francoper Hinterdeich
Francoper Str.
Alter-Deich
Moorburger-
Landscheide
Untenburger Querweg
Pumpwerk
Moorburger-
Hinterdeich
Waltershofer Str.
HEW Abspannwerk Süd
Untenburger Querweg
Pumpwerk
Moorburger-
Georg- Heyken- Str.
E45
7
31
30
HAMBU
Werder Str.
Dradenauer Str.
ProLogis
BUSS Logistik Terminal GmbH
IGS Krohn&Schröder
Finkenwerder Str.
Hauptdeich
Aluminiumwerke
Vollhöfner Weiden
REMAIN TRANS-SAFETY LOCKS
OCEANGATE Distribution
Rangierbahnhof Alte Süderelbe
Cargo Zentrum Hafen Hamburg
Sharp
Kirche
Kirchweg
Altenw.
HH-Wa
1. Untenburger Stieg
2. Grusort
3. Grusortwinkel
4. Obenburger Stieg
5. Neuer Nehusweg
7. Käuzchenstieg
8. Teichhuhnstr.
9. Steinmarderweg
10. Krickentenweg
11. Wieselstr.
12. Schnepfenstieg
13. Wildkatzenweg
14. Räbelkehre
15. Wischenpfad
16. Gehegekamp
17. Gehegestieg
Neu-wieden-thal
Neugraben- Fischbek
Hausbrucher Moor
Beiersdorf Verw.- u. Lager
Beiersdorf AG Werk 4
Neuwiedenthaler Str.
Cuxhavener Str.
73
Neugraben
Neuwiedenthal
Betonwerk
Hausbruch
Scheinberg
Altwiedenthal
Reiherberg
Falkenberg
Fischbek
Neugraben-
Staatsforst Hamburg
Ehestorfer Heuweg
Landhs. Jägerhof
Gasths. Kärtner-Hütte
Revierförsterei
Heykenaukamp
Zum Dubben
Hamburg Moorb